Talk About a Great INVENTION!

By Erin Dealey

Alexander Graham Bell invented the telephone. Read about how his daughter learns about her father's invention.

PEARSON

 This is a play about how the telephone was **invented**. In a play, people have speaking parts that tell a story. Look for each person's name. If you wish, read the name aloud. Read aloud the words that come after the name.

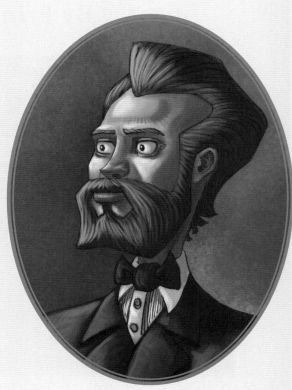

 Daisy Bell was born in 1880.

Alexander Graham Bell invented the telephone in 1876.

This play takes place in 1887. Mr. Bell has already **invented** the telephone. Mr. Bell's daughter Daisy wants to know how her father invented it.

Thomas Watson helped Mr. Bell build his invention.

Mrs. Bell is deaf, but she can read lips.

At Home With Mr. Bell and Daisy

MR. BELL: Daisy, what is the matter? You look quite upset. Tell me what has happened.

DAISY: Father, the boy next door said that you didn't invent the telephone! He said that someone else did.

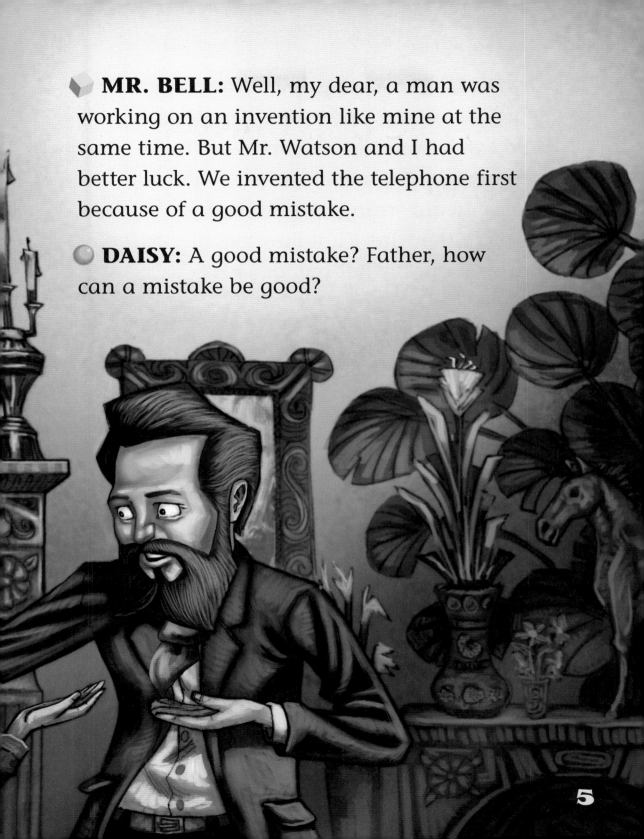

MR. BELL: Well, my dear, a man was working on an invention like mine at the same time. But Mr. Watson and I had better luck. We invented the telephone first because of a good mistake.

DAISY: A good mistake? Father, how can a mistake be good?

5

MR. BELL: A mistake can be good when it leads to a new idea. Mr. Watson and I were working on improving the **telegraph**. But one of the parts got stuck. Then I heard strange sounds coming through the wire. That gave me an idea. Can you guess what my idea was?

DAISY: Yes! Words are sounds. If sounds can come through a **telegraph** wire, so can words. I'm so glad Mr. Watson is coming to lunch tomorrow. I can ask him about the invention, too.

Mr. Bell Greets Mr. Watson

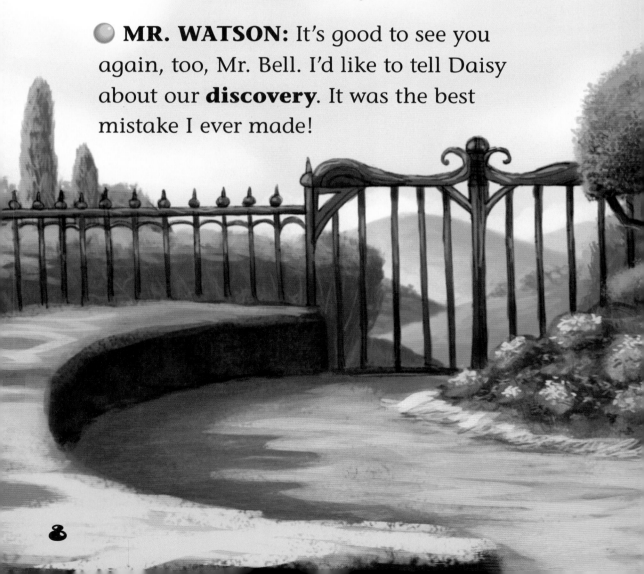

MR. BELL: Thomas, so good to see you again! My daughter Daisy is excited to hear about our **discovery**.

MR. WATSON: It's good to see you again, too, Mr. Bell. I'd like to tell Daisy about our **discovery**. It was the best mistake I ever made!

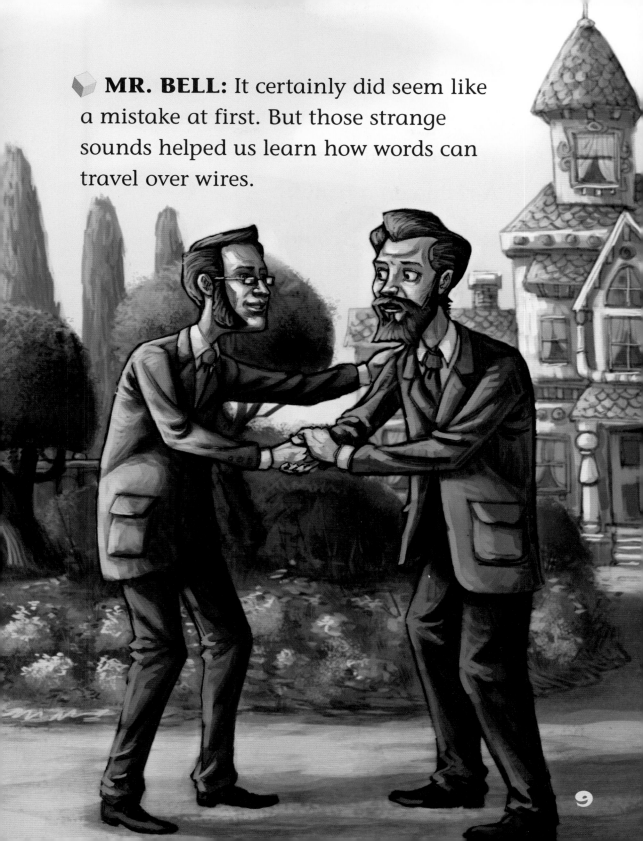

MR. BELL: It certainly did seem like a mistake at first. But those strange sounds helped us learn how words can travel over wires.

MR. WATSON: Do you remember the song I sang to test our first telephone?

Yankee Doodle went to town

A-riding on a pony!

MR. BELL: How could I forget! I discovered that you sing off-key!

Lunch With Mr. Watson

DAISY: Father told me about your good mistake, Mr. Watson. You helped him discover that sounds can come through a wire.

MR. WATSON: Yes. Once we knew how sound could travel over the wires, we knew **speech** could, too. But it took seven more months before we could send speech over the wires.

DAISY: Why did it take so long? Isn't **speech** just sounds?

MR. WATSON: That's hard to explain. Do you play the piano?

DAISY: Yes, I do. Mother is deaf, but she can "hear" me play. She puts her hands on the piano and feels it move.

MR. WATSON: Your mother feels the strings inside the piano **vibrate**. The strings vibrate to make sounds. It took us seven months to make the wires in our telephone vibrate to make speech.

DAISY: So that's how it works! The wires **vibrate** to make words. But a boy told me that someone else made the telephone.

MR. WATSON: Well, another man tried, but we were first. It was March 6, 1876. I was in another room when I heard your father say, "Mr. Watson, come here! I want you!" over the wires.

DAISY: I'm going to tell that boy that you and father invented the telephone because of a good mistake!

MR. WATSON: I like to think my singing helped, too!

Glossary

discovery something found for the first time

invented created a machine or came up with an idea that no one had ever thought of before

speech spoken words

telegraph a machine used long ago to send messages over wires by tapping out a code

vibrate to move back and forth